THE SINKING OF THE USS *MAINE*, 1898

WITH THE ISLAND OF CUBA engaged in a bloody rebellion against Spain in 1898, the American battleship *Maine* was sent to Spanish-controlled Havana to protect United States citizens. The visit was proclaimed as "friendly," though it was no secret that American sympathies were almost wholly on the side of the Cuban rebels. On the night of February 15, under mysterious circumstances, a mighty explosion tore the *Maine* apart, sinking her and killing over 250 of her crew. A court of inquiry determined that the explosion was no accident, but it was unable to fix the blame. Angry and in a crusading mood, Congress soon after declared war on Spain, thereby starting America on her role as a power in world affairs.

PRINCIPALS

THE NEW YORK JOURNAL, the most rabid "yellow journal" of the day, which used every trick of distortion and sensation to influence public opinion and bring on the war.

FITZHUGH LEE, American consul in Havana.

PRESIDENT WILLIAM MCKINLEY, who tried valiantly to avert war, but was forced to bow to prevailing circumstances and the mood of the country.

DUPUY DE LOME, Spanish ambassador to the United States, whose blundering insult against the President created a furor.

THE USS MAINE, the ill-fated ship, pride of the U.S. Navy, whose destruction made war inevitable.

CAPTAIN WILLIAM SAMPSON, chairman of the first naval court of inquiry.

CAPTAIN CHARLES SIGSBEE, commanding officer of the *Maine* and one of the survivors of the tragedy.

PRESIDENT WILLIAM HOWARD TAFT, who issued orders in 1912 to have the wreck of the *Maine* raised from Havana Harbor.

ADMIRAL CHARLES VREELAND, chairman of the court of inquiry in 1912.

THE NAMELESS MEN, who set off the terrible explosion that sank the *Maine*; they were the principal actors in the stark drama.

The *American battleship* USS Maine. *Overhead insert shows her skipper, Captain Charles D. Sigsbee. Commissioned in 1895, she weighed 6,682 tons. Her mainmast was erected as a monument at Arlington National Cemetery in honor of crew members buried there. Her foremast was erected at the United States Naval Academy, Annapolis, Maryland. (National Archives)*

A FOCUS BOOK

The Sinking of the USS *Maine*

February 15, 1898

The Incident that Triggered the Spanish-American War

by John Walsh

FRANKLIN WATTS, INC.

575 Lexington Avenue   New York, N.Y. 10022

Cover photo courtesy of The National Archives

The authors and publishers of the Focus Books wish to acknowledge the
helpful editorial suggestions of Professor Richard B. Morris.

SBN 531-01004-x

Contents

Dedicated to
John B. Kelly
and
Matthew, Ann, Michael, Georgina,
Timothy, Daniel, Thomas,
John, Patrick, Mariann

THE SINKING OF THE USS *MAINE*, 1898

Captain Charles D. Sigsbee, commanding officer of the USS Maine, *and the last to leave the sinking ship. (National Archives)*

In Havana Harbor, 1898

The wide sweep of Havana Harbor lay quiet beneath a heavily overcast sky on the night of February 15, 1898. No moon shone and only the lights of the capital city of Cuba, ringing the low shoreline, pierced the darkness. The easterly trade winds had faded by early evening and there was no breeze to relieve the sultry atmosphere.

On the broad expanse of water, ships large and small loomed darkly as they rode at anchor, yellow warning signals glowing dully at bow and stern, with an occasional light from deck or porthole casting a cheerful gleam. Three of these ships loomed larger than all the others: the American passenger steamer *City of Washington*, which had arrived only the day before; the formidable Spanish battleship *Alfonso XII*; and the newest American battleship, the USS *Maine*.

At that time one of the most impressive fighting ships in existence, the *Maine* was the pride of the United States Navy. The first warship entirely designed and built by American naval architects, she carried heavy armament — a total of twenty-five guns of differing caliber including four big ten-inchers — as well as gear and equipment of high sophistication for that day. Her top speed of seventeen knots placed her among the fastest naval vessels in the world. Even as she swung lazily at anchor in the changing tide, the lines of her steel hull, painted completely white, showed sleek and powerful above the blackened waters.

Aboard the *Maine*, the 350 officers and enlisted men of her crew were relaxing before turning in for the night. Some wrote letters; some read; most simply lounged on deck to escape the stuffiness below. From amidships the music of an accordion and a mandolin rose on the still air, mixed with talking and laughter. In his cabin in the afterpart of the ship, Captain Charles D. Sigsbee, commanding officer of the *Maine*, sat at his desk writing a long overdue letter to his family. Before coming to Havana the *Maine* had been on maneuvers with the North Atlantic Squadron for a month and there had been no time to think about letters.

As Sigsbee wrote, the silvery tones of a bugle suddenly rang out above the music and the labored chugging of a passing ferry. The plaintive sound of taps was the regular announcement to the ship's personnel that another day had ended and it was time for slinging hammocks in the crew's quarters. The Captain put down his pen and listened as note after note echoed hauntingly across the wide harbor. He had heard the sound thousands of times, yet somehow he always paused to listen.

But this night was different. Though no one on board knew it, the bugle was marking much more than the completion of another ordinary day. In reality, it was pronouncing a tragic requiem for the great ship itself and for most of her crew. Even beyond that, all unknowingly, it was proclaiming the start of a new era in American history, the modern era in which America stands as a leader in world

[4]

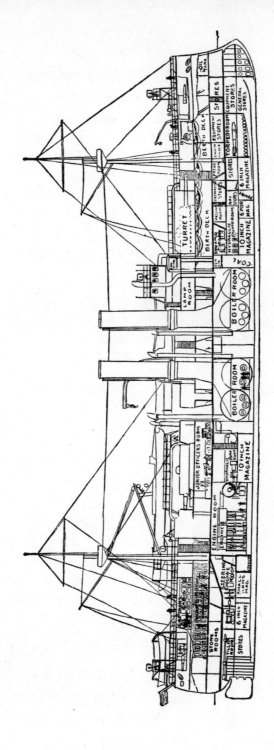

A sectional view of the interior of the battleship Maine. The explosion demolished the forward section from the smokestack to the bow. (New York Public Library)

affairs. For less than an hour after the last strains of the bugle died away, the *Maine* would be a shattered and burned-out hulk on the bottom of Havana Harbor. Her destruction would become the final incident in a train of circumstances that plunged the United States into war with Spain.

Why the *Maine* Was in Cuba

The island of Cuba, situated only ninety miles from Florida, had been a possession of Spain for centuries. A country of almost constant political unrest, Cuba had frequently been racked by revolution, but none of these uprisings had ever come close to ending Spanish rule. In 1895, however, fighting had broken out again. This time it was led by a determined and skillful band of rebels who hoped to enlist the sympathy of the United States in their struggle for independence.

By February of 1898, almost three years of fierce guerrilla warfare had raged across the island, leaving many thousands of Cubans homeless, destitute, or dead. Spain, taking large losses and fighting an enemy that struck swiftly from hiding places in hill and forest, had been forced to build up its troop strength until nearly a quarter of a million Spanish soldiers were under arms on the island. And still the fighting went on, becoming ever more brutal and bloody on both sides. The Spaniards, especially, in their frantic efforts to counter rebel moves, sometimes inflicted excessive retaliation; one commander, General Weyler, earned the unenviable nickname of "The Butcher."

From the beginning, Americans had sympathized with the Cubans' desire for liberty. With the almost daily reports that told of the sufferings of her small island neighbor, the American feeling finally deepened to concern, frustration, even anger. When Spain, striving to pacify the island by breaking up the rebels' supply bases, began a policy of uprooting and shifting large segments of the Cuban people, many Americans heatedly called for military intervention by the United States. Huge supplies of food and clothing were soon flowing from America to relieve the sufferings of the displaced Cubans, the *Reconcentrados*, or "reconcentrated ones." But, despite the aid, the death rate among the *Reconcentrados*, from starvation and disease, was appalling.

The anguish of Cuba, skillfully propagandized by the rebels, could hardly avoid wringing a response from the hearts of Ameri-

Captain Sigsbee at the telephone in his cabin on the Maine. *The cabin was located aft and thus escaped the full impact of the explosion. (New York Public Library)*

cans. But at this very time in the United States there were other, less obvious forces at work which heightened that sympathetic response beyond all expectations.

In 1898, a developing America was standing on the threshold of international involvement; both government and people were ready to look beyond the country's natural boundaries toward a more significant role on the world stage. The far reaches of the vast continent itself had been explored, brought under control, and largely settled. The American economy had expanded fantastically. Internal affairs, despite occasional upheavals, had become more or less stable and for more than thirty years no catastrophic disturbance had marred the nation's progress. Lifting her gaze to view the world scene, the United States could hardly ignore, or fail to be moved by, the plight of Cuba. In a rare combination of national idealism and compassion, Americans began to feel, rightly or wrongly, that they must somehow restore peace to the strife-torn island. A sense of mission took root deep in the nation's heart.

Another important element in this mood, particularly regarding American sympathies toward the rebels, was the incredible part played by some of the newspapers of the time. Without modern day radio, newsreels, or television, the people of 1898 derived most of their knowledge of world affairs from the columns of newspapers. And, it was just at this time that a radically different concept of journalism had taken hold. Instead of reporting the news objectively and truthfully, many papers strove to provide frequent, even daily, sensations in a misguided attempt to boost readership. When real sensations were not available, these papers did not hesitate to distort facts and twist meanings, or to foster false controversy in bold, ever-enlarging headlines. The situation in Cuba was a prime source for stories of gripping human interest and startling political developments, and in these stories, Spain was inevitably cast in the role of villain. The result was an orgy of bad and frantic journalism. Although it was decried by many, it still had a great emotional effect on readers and made such newspapers a potent weapon in the formation of public opinion.

The chief offender and best example of this "yellow journalism," as it came to be called, was William Randolph Hearst's New York *Journal*, then vying with the New York *World* for circulation supremacy. The *Journal*, in fact, went so far in manufacturing and warping the news, and in expressing its blatant hatred for Spain, that many historians today agree the paper played a major role in arousing Americans to a warlike attitude.

By 1898, the feeling between the United States and Spain had settled into a quiet, mutual antagonism, with Yankee sentiment almost entirely on the side of the Cuban insurrectionists. There was still an American consul in Cuba, however, and many Americans continued to conduct business there in safety. Early in January, though, some rioting occurred in Havana, and while it soon quieted down, uneasiness and tension remained. The result was a decision by the United States to dispatch a warship to the city to provide a place of refuge for Americans in the event of serious trouble. There seems also to have been some hope that such a "friendly" visit, in which all the traditional amenities were strictly observed, might help to lessen the strain between the two countries.

Uncertain whether the Spanish authorities in Cuba would permit the intrusion of an American vessel, even on a friendly mission, the U.S. government decided on a stratagem: word of the intended visit would be sent only at the last moment. Accordingly, on January 24, the American consul in Havana, Fitzhugh Lee, an ex-Confederate Army officer, was alerted by cable that the *Maine* would

[9]

be arriving the next day, and that he was to inform the Spanish authorities. The *Maine* was already on the high seas and, without a radio, could not be recalled even if the Spaniards objected. At eleven o'clock on the morning of January 25, the proud ship, her gleaming white hull topped by the varnished surface of the wood-and-metal superstructure, arrived off Havana and slowed to take on the Spanish harbor pilot.

Entry into the harbor was without incident, though not without some tension because of the *Maine*'s sudden arrival and doubts about the kind of reception that might be in store. As the ship steamed slowly under the guns of Morro Castle, at the harbor entrance, the crew casually took up positions in the vicinity of battle stations. Sigsbee wanted them on the alert, but wished to avoid any appear-

The Maine *entering Havana Harbor on January 25, 1898. Uncertain about the reception he and his ship would receive, Captain Sigsbee had the crew on the alert near battle stations. To the right is Morro Castle, the Spanish fortress.(National Archives)*

ance of belligerence; to those watching from the land the crewmen appeared to be merely lounging on deck. Within the harbor the *Maine* came up to her assigned berth, about 400 yards from the nearest shore, and was moored. Shortly after, a case of sherry, sent by the disgruntled Spanish commander more as a formality than as a token of welcome, arrived on board and everyone relaxed.

During the next few days Sigsbee and his officers paid various official courtesy calls on the Spaniards and even attended a bullfight in Havana. But as a precaution all such visits were kept to a minimum and the crew was not granted liberty at all. Sigsbee wanted no chance encounters between the *Maine*'s personnel and the excitable Spanish residents of the city, some of whom, he realized, would inevitably see the formidable vessel as a veiled threat. While he was at the bullfight, in fact, there had been thrust into his hand a printed broadside labeling the *Maine*'s presence in Havana "an insult." In such a situation, loose words and ill temper might easily spark real trouble and this Sigsbee meant to avoid at all costs.

Through early February the vessel rode peacefully at anchor, without incident. Once or twice officers visiting ashore on official calls were met by hostile remarks from Spanish civilians, but that was to be expected and it prompted no concern. By February 8, the *Maine* had been in Cuban waters for two weeks, and with the atmosphere back in the United States grown calmer, it was thought the time had come to terminate the visit. But this was not to be. Fate, in the person of the Spanish ambassador to Washington, intervened.

Dupuy De Lome, the Spanish envoy, was usually a man of great discretion but now he committed the first blunder of his career and it was a costly one. Writing a private letter to a friend in Cuba, he unguardedly expressed some insults against President McKinley. He also implied that Spain, instead of trying to halt the bloodshed in Cuba, was only placating American opinion until she could launch a major attack on the rebels. The letter was somehow stolen by the insurrectionists who, recognizing its tremendous propaganda value, quickly made it available to the newspapers. On February 9, the news broke. Among other insults, De Lome had written that McKinley was "weak and catering to the rabble and, besides, a low politician who desires to leave the door open to himself and to stand well with the jingoes of his party." Despite the fact that it was a private letter, De Lome was a Spanish official and American anger boiled over.

During the following week stories about De Lome and his letter filled the front pages. At first he denied writing it; then he admitted that he had, and offered to resign. Not satisfied with this, Congress demanded an official apology from Spain and a clarification of its military policy in Cuba. Spain, in turn, rebuffed the U.S. Congress by insisting that De Lome's resignation was sufficient. This failure to publicly disavow De Lome's statements deepened the already dangerous situation. On the morning of February 15, the *New York Times*, reporting the Spanish refusal, headlined: SPAIN DEFIES AMERICA. And that very night in Havana Harbor the *Maine* came to her terrible and mysterious end.

A Night of Tragedy and Horror

Aboard the *Maine*, by 9:30 P.M., the music had stopped and the vessel was wrapped in silence. A few men were standing their regular watches but most of the crew were asleep in their hammocks, which were slung row upon row two decks below in the crew's quarters forward. Captain Sigsbee, still writing at his desk in the dull glare of a feeble electric light, was putting the finishing touches on the letter to his family.

On its western side, the land ringing Havana Harbor rises to a hill of moderate height. Here, a young man out for an evening's stroll paused to look down on the ships that dotted the water, their riding lights hovering like fireflies in the dark. As he gazed at the scene, so like a painting in its dark serenity, with a shattering suddenness there burst on his ears a thunderous roar, and the ground under his feet momentarily trembled. Shaken by the massive concussion, this eyewitness stared aghast as there erupted from the

Captain Sigsbee in his cabin. He was sitting at this same table, writing a letter to his wife, when the ship blew up. (New York Public Library)

Maine a monstrous inferno of smoke and flame. The ship heaved crazily as a vast column of slate-colored smoke, eerily lit by the fire, churned upward hundreds of feet into the air, then flattened outward to form a great rolling canopy over the stricken vessel. Swiftly, the cloud of smoke continued to spread until it overhung the entire harbor.

It seemed to the horrified young man that the *Maine*'s bow section had been completely torn apart — its beams and plating smashed and twisted, decks ripped open, wood and metal crushed into a nightmarish mass of destruction. In hypnotized disbelief, he continued to watch as the dying vessel writhed in the raging flames and trembled under the onslaught of the inrushing harbor waters and the collapsing superstructure.

In his cabin, Captain Sigsbee had been about to place his letter in an envelope when the explosion occurred. As he later described it, he heard a "bursting, rending and crashing sound or roar of immense volume." He felt the deck lurch beneath him, first tipping at the bow and then listing strongly to port. Almost immediately there followed a "succession of heavy, ominous metallic sounds and reverberations," caused by the tumbling of smokestacks and masts and the falling of huge pieces of debris that had been blown high into the air with the smoke.

The lights of the cabin had flicked out within seconds of the initial explosion, acrid smoke had filled the room, and Sigsbee was left standing in the choking darkness, gripped by the sudden thought that the ship was about to capsize and carry him under. For a moment he thought only of saving himself, but his long years of command experience quickly took control and he brushed aside all thought of his own welfare.

The USS Maine *at her berth in Havana Harbor. She lay about four hundred yards from shore, and the explosion shattered many of the windows in the buildings along the wharves. (New York Public Library)*

Arms outstretched, Sigsbee was groping his way in the blackness along the listing passageway, when he bumped violently into someone going in the opposite direction. It was Marine Private William Anthony, Sigsbee's orderly, who with no thought for his own safety was going belowdecks in search of his superior. Legend usually pictures Private Anthony at this moment as drawing to attention, saluting, and saying, in the old Navy manner, some such words as, "Sir, I have the honor to report that the ship is blown up and is sinking." But the truth, as later recorded by Sigsbee himself, had no such comic opera touch. The story was, in fact, nothing but the invention of a newspaper reporter. In reality, after Anthony identified himself, both men hastened out of the passageway onto the chaotic main deck. Here Sigsbee suddenly realized that he had no idea at what time the explosion occurred, and that he would need this information for his report. He inquired the exact time of Anthony, who replied: "The explosion took place at 9:40, sir. I looked at the clock a few minutes ago."

With anxious eyes Sigsbee peered toward the bow, but could make out only a grotesque dark mass of twisted metal rising high overhead, around which flames licked hungrily. He was stunned at the sight; it seemed as if the whole bow had been doubled back on itself. Glancing down he saw that the water was lapping over his shoes as it crept slowly up the slanting deck.

Turning, Sigsbee carefully picked his way aft over the debris to the poop deck, the highest open space on the ship. Here he found two or three other officers already gathered and trying to assess the damage. None of the sleeping crew had yet appeared, Sigsbee was told, and all efforts to investigate forward had been blocked by the flames and the rising water. Then a new fire suddenly flared up amidships, casting a fitful light over the adjacent waters, in which

[16]

An imaginative drawing of the explosion, published in the New York World, *February 16, 1898. The actual moment was much more devastating than the artist has shown. (New York Public Library)*

Sigsbee could dimly make out floating forms. Some drifted lifelessly but others appeared to be making feeble efforts to stay above the surface; cries and groans rose weakly from the water.

Hurriedly the commanding officer asked what lifeboats were serviceable, and discovered that only two could be manned. These he ordered put into the water to pick up survivors but refused to enter one himself. Though he was aware by this time that the *Maine* was going down fast, he was unwilling to abandon his ship until the last possible moment. As the men struggled to get the lifeboats free, another hazard appeared: some ammunition stored above decks began exploding from the heat of the flames.

Now other men stumbled out on deck. One, a midshipman, scrambled aft away from the fire, dazed but uninjured. He had been below when the explosion occurred and the deck on which he was standing had simply split beneath his feet, dropping him into hip-deep water on the deck below. Searching frantically for a way out, he thought he was finished until he felt a sudden blast of air: looking up he was amazed to find that the side of the ship had been blown away. Another seaman, two decks below at the moment of the disaster, was lifted by the blast through the ripped-open decks above him and came down in the water beside the ship amid flaming wreckage. Oblivious of a dislocated hip and a broken shoulder, he ducked under the burning surface and swam for his life.

For most of the others below it was a more tragic story. In the crew's quarters the sleeping men were thrown in every direction and those who retained consciousness, or were not killed outright, found themselves in total darkness with the deck pitching and tilting at impossible angles. Frantic efforts to gain the safety of the upper decks were often blocked by wreckage and the mounting water.

The few men on deck were luckier, but even some of these

escaped death only by a miracle. One Marine sergeant, on watch at the gangway, was blown so high by the concussion that he had a momentary view of the whole ship. On the way down, he landed on an awning and crashed through it. Opening his eyes a few moments later he found himself sprawled on the deck, bruised but not seriously hurt. Another sailor, on duty beside the forward ten-inch-gun turret, was flung headlong from the ship along with the turret itself; man and turret hit the water simultaneously. Dragged under by the turbulent suction, the man fought his way to the surface and was later picked up, choking for breath but still alive. One lucky sailor who had chosen to sling his hammock on deck was hurled into the water a full fifty yards from the ship, sustaining only a gash on the head.

Captain Sigsbee, standing on the poop deck, continued to gaze hopefully for signs of life on board. Then, in the flickering light cast by the fires, he noted with relief that other boats had arrived to help: they came from shore and from the steamer *City of Washington*, as well as from the Spanish warship *Alfonso* and most of the other ships in the harbor. One of the *Maine*'s own boats, after searching for about fifteen minutes, now returned with the information that all survivors and dead that could be spotted had been picked up. It was time, the officers urged, for Sigsbee to leave the *Maine*.

The Captain hesitated, wondering again if it would be possible to penetrate forward and look for any survivors still aboard, but he finally had to admit this would be impossible. The bow was already largely submerged and fires still burned in the parts above water. The ammunition, too, was still periodically going off, hurling missiles haphazardly into the night, and no one could tell whether another large explosion might not take place at any moment. In any case, the entire ship would soon be going under; the sloping poop deck upon which Sigsbee stood was already nearly on a level with the water. Sigsbee ordered the two officers still with him into the boat and then stepped in himself. His manner was calm and he appeared cool, but as one of the men later remarked, his face looked ten years older.

As the last boat pulled away from the sinking vessel, a high-pitched, piercing sound — made by air being forced from water-tight compartments — filled the night with a weird noise, like the wailing of troubled spirits. Glancing back, Sigsbee watched sadly as his ship settled slowly beneath the surface. Moments later the *Maine*'s keel gently touched the muddy bottom of the harbor, leaving only twisted portions of the superstructure and the intact after-mast still visible. The last crackling flame was extinguished and the rain, which had been threatening all evening, finally began to fall.

Informed that many of the injured had been taken aboard the *City of Washington*, Sigsbee decided to head there first. At least, he thought, on the big steamer he would be on United States "territory" and amid all the uncertainty and confusion about the cause of the blast, he and his men would feel more secure. Aboard the *City of Washington* Sigsbee was quickly taken to the large salon, where he was appalled by the sight that met his eyes.

Around the salon, some twenty of the *Maine*'s crew lay sprawled on tables and couches or were stretched out on mattresses that had been hastily flung on the floor. Many of the men were badly hurt, with ugly burns or bloody wounds showing through torn clothing. Around them doctors and aides, with many women volunteers, worked feverishly. To each man in turn Sigsbee spoke a word of encouragement and made sure he was being looked after. Then he instructed one of his officers to conduct a muster of all hands, sending messengers to other ships and ashore where necessary, to determine how many men had been hurt or killed and how many were still unaccounted for.

It was now about 10:30 P.M., almost an hour since the explosion. With nothing further demanding his immediate attention, Sigsbee realized it was time to report the disaster to his superiors in the Navy Department. He wondered how he should word his message, knowing that whatever he said would speedily become public knowledge. He must be clear and precise, but he must also be careful to offer no fuel for public hysteria. On a piece of the steamer's own stationery he wrote in pencil:

Secnav
Washington, D.C.

Maine blown up in Havana harbor at nine-forty tonight and destroyed. Many wounded and doubtless many more killed or

Some of the wounded crewmen of the Maine, *in a hospital at Key West, Florida. They were among the lucky one third who survived. (New York Public Library)*

drowned. Wounded and others on board Spanish Man of War and Ward Line steamer. Send Lighthouse tenders from Key West for crew and the few pieces of equipment above water. No one has clothing other than that upon him. Public opinion should be suspended until further report...

Sigsbee was well aware that nothing could influence the public to suspend its opinion entirely, especially in the midst of the bitterness over the De Lome letter. A large portion of the public would inevitably hold Spain responsible for the tragedy, and much wild talk of retribution and war would probably fill the air. President McKinley must offer something to cool emotions and Sigsbee was the only man in those first hours who could supply it. Patience and reason, he cautioned, must not be overcome by fear and anger. Satisfied that he had said all he could for the moment, he added the information that all officers had been saved, then signed his name. As he finished, a group of Spanish officials filed slowly into the room.

Solemn-faced, they approached Sigsbee and assured him of their profound sympathies. They had been sent by the Governor-General, they explained, and were ready to provide all possible assistance; Sigsbee had only to direct them. Such a prompt and generous offer, Sigsbee thought, would help to soothe American tempers, so he took up his pencil again and added to his message: "Many Spanish officers, including representatives of General Blanco now with me to express sympathy." Again he signed his name, sealed up the dispatch, and sent it ashore to be transmitted by cable.

The Spaniards talked quietly for a few moments, then voiced the question that was on everyone's mind: what did Sigsbee think had caused the explosion? Unhesitatingly he replied that he did not know and that he was not free to discuss the question before an

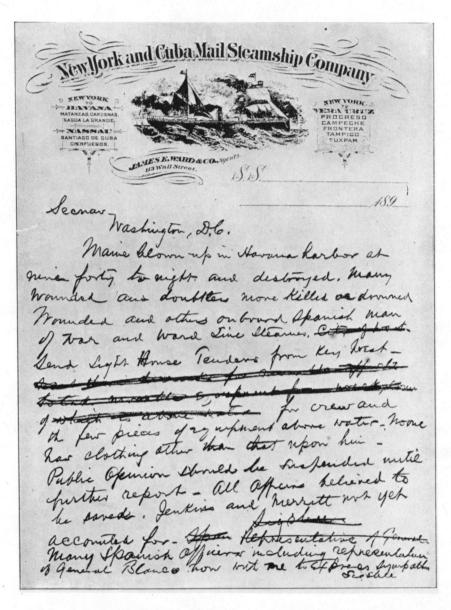

The message sent by Captain Sigsbee to the Secretary of the Navy in Washington less than an hour after the explosion. It was cabled from Havana and was in President McKinley's hands about midnight. (National Archives)

investigation had been made by his government. At this, one of the Spaniards, a general of distinguished military bearing, stepped forward and earnestly declared that the Spanish forces in Cuba knew nothing whatever about the incident and could not be implicated in any way in such an appalling tragedy. Sigsbee thanked him and repeated that he was placing no blame. Satisfied, the Spaniards departed.

Despite what he had said, however, Sigsbee did have thoughts of his own about the explosion, though he had no notion at all as to who was involved. A few minutes later he wrote another dispatch, this one to be sent to the government in secret the next day, by way of Key West:

Maine was probably destroyed by a mine. It may have been done by accident. I surmise that her berth was planted previous to her arrival; perhaps long ago. I can only surmise this.

It was near midnight when the officer who had been sent to take the muster returned. His report revealed the full horror of the evening's events. Of the 350 officers and men who had been on board, only 98 were still alive, and only 16 of these had escaped without injury. The dreadful total of 252 men had perished, most of them entombed in the wreckage of the *Maine*. Subsequently, 8 more men died of their wounds, bringing the final death count to 260.

The charred wreckage of the Maine's superstructure the day after the explosion. At left, an inspection team approaches. (National Archives)

How Could It Have Happened?

The cable sent by Sigsbee to the Secretary of the Navy reached Washington sometime after midnight and was taken immediately to the President. McKinley, awakened from a sound sleep, at first could only repeat the startling message incredulously: "The *Maine* blown up! The *Maine* blown up!" As he dressed, he ordered messengers sent to convene his Cabinet officers and aides, and within half an hour an emergency meeting was underway behind locked doors. Shortly afterward a horde of newspaper reporters besieged the White House and as the morning of February 16 dawned, Americans read the shocking news from Havana.

Most papers treated the sensational development soberly, making an attempt to stay within the available facts, expressing only guarded opinion. The *New York Times*, for example, printed a straight headline of only four words — THE MAINE BLOWN UP — and the accompanying story stressed the fact that the cause of the tragedy had not yet been determined. Then, the next day, the paper dutifully reported that all indications pointed to the cause being an accident, although it did admit that the situation was uncertain and full of danger. The *Times* went on to supply a roundup of official opinion which occupied the entire second page and which bore the lengthy heading: "Public men recognize its gravity if it is found that the disaster was not an accident."

The "yellow press," however, led by Hearst's New York *Journal*, lost all sense of editorial proportion. Ignoring Captain Sigsbee's plea that the public be kept calm, the *Journal* printed a carefully crafted headline deliberately calculated to excite and mislead readers. Spread across the entire front page was this:

CRISIS IS AT HAND 253 KNOWN TO BE LOST
CABINET IN SESSION; GROWING BELIEF IN
DE LOME IN PANIC, FLEES SPANISH TREACHERY

A smaller headline on the same page stated that some naval officers were of the opinion that the *Maine* had been sunk by "an outside attack." The next day, still lacking any evidence whatsoever, the *Journal's* headline hysteria continued:

WAR! SURE!
MAINE DESTROYED BY SPANISH; THIS PROVED ABSOLUTELY BY DISCOVERY OF THE
TORPEDO HOLE

[27]

The same issue carried a large drawing, spread over the entire upper half of the page, showing the *Maine* anchored above a floating mine. The picture was pure imagination, meant to show how the explosion might have been accomplished, but many undiscerning readers accepted it as fact.

The New York *World*, trying its best to match the sensational effects of the *Journal*'s distortions while keeping within the bounds of reason, offered a huge sketch of the *Maine* at the moment of the explosion. The headline proclaimed: NOT AN ACCIDENT, SIGSBEE SAYS. Evidently, the "secret" message in which Sigsbee had stated his belief that the ship "was probably destroyed by a mine" was no longer a secret. But the *World* had twisted Sigsbee's careful words to suit its own purposes: the Captain had actually said that while there might have been a mine involved, it *still* could have been an accident.

Most level-headed people, though understandably astounded, confused, and angry, quietly awaited further developments. What could Spain hope to achieve, they wondered, by blowing up the *Maine* and killing most of her crew? Such a senseless act, if it proved to be true, would almost certainly lead to war, and Spain had already shown how far she would go to avoid conflict with the United States. It was possible, of course, that some rabid faction of Spaniards, acting independently, might have done the deed, but nothing could be known for certain until an investigation had taken place.

The Investigation Begins

Acting swiftly, President McKinley appointed a naval court of inquiry, whose orders were to proceed without delay to Havana. It consisted of four officers of wide experience: Captains William Sampson and Henry Chadwick, and Lieutenant Commanders Adolph Marix and William Potter. With Sampson, a future admiral, in charge, the court arrived in Cuba on February 20 and set up headquarters aboard the *Mangrove*, a small cruiser anchored near the *Maine*. As it began its deliberations the next day, less than a week after the explosion, the sun shone serenely over the glistening waters of the harbor, providing a deceptively cheerful setting. But as one reporter wrote: "The wreck is the central figure of an otherwise bright picture and it is as sad as it is terrible."

It was up to the court to determine both the cause of the disaster and who was responsible for it. To do this it arranged to question a long list of people: all survivors of the blast as well as any volunteer eyewitnesses from the shore and from other ships. In addition, experienced U.S. Navy divers would be sent down to examine every inch of the *Maine*.

If the explosion had been an accident, it was realized, certain very definite causes would have to be involved. The *Scientific American* for February 26 provided avid readers with the following clear explanation of these possibilities:

The accidental cause may have arisen from fire, due to spontaneous combustion of coal in the bunkers, or from a short-circuited wire, or there may have been an explosion due to the decomposition of the high explosives on board. There are coal bunkers on three sides of the ten-inch magazine, and it has happened more than once that fires have occurred in the bunkers of our warships which have become fierce enough before they were discovered to make the steel plates inclosing the bunkers red hot. The brown powder, however, of which the ten-inch ammunition is made up, can be heated to nearly 600 degrees F. with impunity, and the gun-cotton of the torpedoes can only be exploded by detonation. There remains the theory that the boiler, which was supplying the electric light dynamos, exploded and set off the magazines. This would fully account for the double reports spoken of in many of the accounts by eyewitnesses. If this was the cause of the disaster, it will be a difficult matter to prove from the appearance of the wreck whether the boiler or the magazine was the first to explode.

Thus, for the accident theory there were four possibilities: a spontaneous fire in the coal bunkers; a bursting of the ship's boilers due to excessive pressure; or a defect in the electrical system — any one of which might have set off the piles of sensitive ammunition stored in the magazines near the bow on the lowest deck; or, last, the ammunition itself might have undergone chemical decomposition and detonated of its own accord.

[30]

Day after day a parade of witnesses appeared before the court on the *Mangrove* providing detailed replies to the searching questions posed by the four officers sitting behind a long, cloth-covered table. Gradually, from this intensive probing, there emerged a picture of the internal conditions on board the *Maine* during the hours prior to the disaster. It began to appear highly doubtful that any of the accident theories would hold up. The coal had been inspected shortly before the explosion, it was claimed by a number of men, and there had been no sign of excessive heat in the bunkers. Other witnesses insisted that the only boilers in operation at the time of the blast were the two in the afterpart of the ship; the forward boilers, in fact, had been closed down for the night. Nor had the electrical system revealed any signs of malfunctioning; all lights and circuits, according to witnesses, had been operating smoothly until the very moment of the explosion. As for the ammunition itself, that, too, had been given its regular evening inspection, with nothing found amiss.

Meanwhile, the divers, working steadily from dawn to dusk in the murky waters around the *Maine*, had not had an easy time. The bow of the vessel had been completely torn asunder and lay sprawled on the bottom, a jungle of twisted metal. Their job was to gather detailed information and relay it to waiting experts on the *Mangrove*, who would attempt to fit the pieces together. In particular, the divers were instructed to make a very careful inspection of the ship's bottom plating, to see in which direction the heavy steel had been bent. If any of these plates sloped inward, toward the interior of the ship, it would be a strong indication, perhaps even proof, that the explosion had originated outside or underneath the vessel.

What the Divers Found

Day after day the divers donned their bulky underwater suits and large metal helmets and were lowered beside the ruined hulk. Cumbersome air hoses restricted their range and hampered their movements, and they had to exercise extreme care while climbing among the jagged chunks and slivers of metal. Despite these difficulties, after about a week's diving three striking facts were established.

First, some of the bottom plating was undeniably bent inward. Second, beneath the point at which the explosion had probably occurred there was a large crater in the muddy floor of the harbor; it was about five feet deep and ten feet across. Third, and most startling of all, the keel of the ship had been bent sharply upward at the point of the blast, actually splitting the *Maine* in two. The severed parts of the ship — the shattered bow and the relatively undamaged after section — rose along the keel to meet in something like an inverted **V**. What could possibly have caused such a distortion, the experts asked, except some great force coming from under the ship's bottom?

Official sketch provided by the naval court of inquiry, based on the descriptions of the divers, showing the demolished bow section underwater. (New York Public Library)

Although the divers' findings went far toward ruling out an accident, the court continued methodically to weigh all of the evidence; momentous issues depended upon its findings and there must be nothing left open to doubt. Many authorities, especially demolition experts, were asked to study the condition of the ship and were then questioned closely and at length by the court. One of these experts, for instance, a Navy veteran of forty years' service named G. A. Converse, was asked: "To what kind of explosion do you attribute the force that caused this bending of plates and keel?" Speaking deliberately, Converse replied: "I am of the opinion that it could be produced by the explosion of a submarine mine, not in contact with the ship, but some distance below it, perhaps on the bottom."

Showing Converse a sketch of the *Maine's* slanting keel, drawn to the divers' specifications, the court inquired: "Could this part have become so distorted from the effects of an *internal* explosion alone?" Converse answered: "I do not think it could. I have never seen anything in my experience which would lead me to believe it is possible." Finally the court put the question to him simply and directly: "Do you think there *must* have been an underwater mine to produce these explosions?" Converse chose his answer with care, leaving out the word *mine*, in order to allow for other possibilities: "Indications are that an underwater explosion produced the conditions." All the other witnesses agreed with Converse's estimate and the final conclusion seemed inescapable: a charge of explosive had somehow been detonated under the *Maine*. But who had done it, and why?

It was Captain Sigsbee himself who provided a starting point for speculation. The ship, he said, had not been over the site of the blast at any other time during her stay in Havana. "On the night of the explosion," as he explained later, "she was pointing in a direction opposite to that in which she had swung throughout the whole previous period." During the hours before the disaster, he said, the *Maine*, while anchored by the bow, had drifted around an arc of 180 degrees.

This seemed to rule out any theory that a mine had been planted on the harbor bottom, since the alleged perpetrators could not be sure that the vessel would swing into position above it. Yet even this was not certain, since the *Maine*'s berth, or mooring area, might have been planted with a *number* of mines before her arrival. And in this connection a pertinent fact was recalled: the Spanish themselves had assigned the ship to its berth and had provided the harbor pilot that brought the vessel in. But had there been enough time for the Spanish to lay the mines in place? After all, they had been informed of the *Maine*'s impending visit only the day before she reached Havana. This was a telling point but not unanswerable. Might not the Spaniards have learned *in advance*, through their

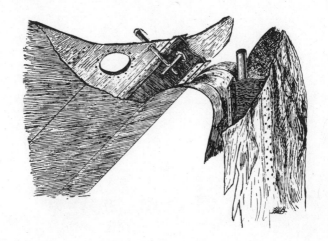

Official close-up drawing of the shattered keel, prepared from sketches made by one of the divers. (New York Public Library)

agents in Washington, of the American government's decision to send the *Maine?* Furthermore, it might not have been a mine at all that caused the explosion. Conceivably, it could have been an electric torpedo, aimed and fired from another ship or from a shore installation, or even some other form of high explosive such as dynamite. Indeed, the ship had lain exposed in the harbor for twenty nights, ample time for any number of schemes to have been hatched and carried out under cover of darkness. The fact that regular watches patrolled the decks at night was no guarantee that all plotters, on or under the blackened waters, would have been detected.

The Coming of War

The court had now been deliberating for nearly a month, while Americans anxiously awaited the results. And the wait was not an entirely uneventful one, for the yellow press had stepped up its campaign of factual distortion — adding to it a bald condemnation of all those in the government who called for patience. Due to the country's apprehensive mood, the strident voices of such papers as the *Journal* and the *World* attained a false urgency that hypnotized readers and sent circulations soaring. All through February and March, for instance, the *Journal* berated President McKinley and his Cabinet for not becoming openly aggressive in their attitude toward Spain. The government was on the side of Wall Street, the paper charged in a vicious and unfounded attack, and was allowing its friends to pile up profits through speculation. The President, ranted the *Journal*, was "ready to surrender every particle of national honor and dignity."

McKinley ignored all this and maintained an attitude of dignity befitting his position and the seriousness of the situation. He did not ignore, however, the secret advance reports that had begun to filter back from Havana early in March, indicating that the accident theory was starting to appear doubtful, and that the explosion might actually have been triggered by a mine. This was very grave indeed and McKinley now recognized that he must prepare the country for the possibility of war; if war did come he did not want America to be caught unprepared.

Peace had reigned in the United States for a generation — since the end of the Civil War — and in the intervening time the Army and Navy had dwindled until they were no more than token forces. The Army had only about thirty thousand men under arms, while smaller Spain had a standing force of nearly half a million. The American Navy, though it had made an attempt (especially by dedicated naval officers) to maintain a strong defensive posture, was still undermanned and ill equipped for a full-scale sea offensive. The need for immediate action was admitted by everyone, including members of Congress, many of whom expressed the belief that a strong United States was the best way to *avoid* war. Spain, though not in a class with America, might still be tempted to defy a country unprepared; certainly she would hesitate before an America fully armed and ready to take the field.

On March 8, amid great excitement, the House of Representatives met to consider a military appropriations bill, requested by McKinley, for fifty million dollars — an enormous sum for the time. Public interest in the scheduled debate ran high and the galleries of the House were packed, while thousands of people surged through the corridors and around the building. Presenting the bill on the floor of the House, Congressman Joseph Cannon stressed the fact that it was not to be considered as a threat to any nation; it was not in any sense a declaration of warlike intentions. "It is not a war appropria-

[37]

tion," he stated emphatically. "I say that in my judgment it is a peace measure. The United States would not, if it could, entrench upon the rights of any nation on earth."

Shouts rang out for an immediate vote, from members confident of a quick passage, but a delay was allowed in order to give time for comment and discussion. Some four hours later, after a dozen ringing speeches had drawn repeated cheers and applause from the spectators, the bill came to a vote and was passed without a single dissenting voice. None of the speakers had leveled an accusing finger at Spain, but rather had confined themselves to statements of patriotic principle. A curious sidelight was the way in which many speakers expressed joy and satisfaction at seeing both north and south firmly united once more — a sign that the scars of the Civil War had perhaps finally healed. On the following day, the Senate added its own unanimous consent to the bill.

The move, as it turned out, was a fortunate and timely one, for with the publication on March 21 of the naval court's findings, events began a headlong, perhaps inevitable, rush toward war. The report, first submitted to the President and then released to the newspapers, set forth in elaborate detail the results of the month-long probe.

Shock and anger swept through America in the wake of the news from Havana. Thousands of young men, moved by patriotic fervor and not waiting to be called, volunteered for military service. Although no one knew what had caused the explosion, many people felt that war would follow. (New York Public Library)

The Findings of the Naval Court

Conditions on the *Maine* itself, the report stated, were excellent. All safety regulations had been strictly enforced at all times. This had even included the wearing of special soft-soled shoes by men entering the ammunition magazines to avoid the possibility of striking sparks from the metal decks. The magazines themselves had been inspected only an hour before the explosion, after which the doors had been secured with locks, and the keys returned to Captain Sigsbee. The divers had found these very keys inside the hulk exactly where Sigsbee had placed them. One of the magazines, it is true, had been found unduly hot during the inspection, but that one was in the afterpart of the ship and had not even blown up; the divers had found it intact. All combustible matter, such as varnish, alcohol, and dangerous wastes, had been stored above decks, as stipulated by Navy regulations, and could have played no part in the explosion.

Moreover, the report went on, there had been no sign of spontaneous combustion in the coal bunkers. Four of the bunkers, in fact, had been empty and one only half full. The only full bunker, the one nearest the magazines, had been inspected about eight o'clock on the night of the disaster and found to be at acceptable temperature, with the coal properly stored. The fire alarms in all the bunkers, it was further explained, had all been tested and found in working order. The boilers were also eliminated as a possible cause: the four boilers near the bow had been discovered in the wreck, knocked out of position but undamaged. They had not burst in any way.

"There were two explosions of a distinctly different character," the report stated, "with a very short but distinct interval between them." The first explosion was sharp and brief, the second more prolonged and of immensely greater volume. It was this second blast, caused by the detonating of the two forward ammunition magazines, that had inflicted the greatest destruction and had caused the ship to sink. It had been of such stupendous force that the heavy steel upper decks at the bow had actually been curled up and back toward the rear of the ship, "folding the forward part of the middle superstructure over and on top of the after part." The report also described the inverted **V** condition of the keel, adding that the point of the break now was only about six feet below the surface of the water, while the rest of the keel sloped down and rested on the bottom, thirty feet below.

The final conclusions of the court were brief and to the point:

The Court finds that the loss of the Maine *on the occasion named was not in any respect due to fault or negligence on the part of the officers or men of the crew of said vessel.*

In the opinion of the Court the Maine *was destroyed by the explosion of a submarine mine, which caused the partial explosion of two of her forward magazines.*

[41]

The Court has been unable to obtain evidence fixing the re-sponsibility for the destruction of the Maine *upon any person or persons.*

The American Reaction: "To Hell with Spain—Remember the *Maine*"

These conclusions, not wholly unexpected of course, sparked the waiting public into an emotional decision of its own. Forgotten was the court's admission that, despite all its careful efforts, it had not succeeded in discovering the perpetrators. People only knew that the USS *Maine*, an American naval vessel, had been blown up in a harbor under Spanish control — deliberately and ruthlessly destroyed along with her crew. All the frustration, suspicion, re-sentment, and disgust that had been building up for the previous three years now broke in a flood of national anger. If the court could not fix the blame, then inflamed public opinion would. Around the country a cry went up that was to become a part of American his-tory: "To hell with Spain — remember the *Maine*!"

Little attention was paid by anyone to the decision of a Spanish court of inquiry which had also been deliberating in Havana. This court insisted that all its questioning of witnesses led to only one possibility: that the explosion was an accident, caused by some in-ternal fault. But this opinion was based entirely on doubtful infer-ences from such things as an absence of dead or stunned fish on the surface of the water around the ship, and a denial by some that any

[42]

Captain Sigsbee aboard the Fern, *one of the assisting vessels, shortly after the explosion. He is in civilian clothes because his uniforms went down with the* Maine. Tom, *the* Maine's *mascot, was rescued from the sinking battleship. (New York Public Library)*

William McKinley, President of the United States, who guided America's diplomatic efforts to bring peace to Cuba while trying to avoid war with Spain.

water had been thrown up by the first blast. The Spanish did not have access to the wreck nor did they question any of the Americans involved. As a consequence, their report was completely ignored.

Considering the mood of the country, if the American court had been able to implicate Spain, then war would probably have come within a matter of days. As it was, however, the element of official uncertainty caused the American government's reaction to veer slightly in another direction. The fighting in Cuba, it was decided, must be stopped without delay and Spain must be forced to grant the island her independence. An aroused America was no longer willing to tolerate what it now firmly believed was purely a

[44]

bloody suppression of liberty, and a good many people loudly declared in favor of actual military intervention.

Thus, while the sinking of the *Maine* was not the direct cause of the Spanish–American War, it was the incident which triggered the final confrontation. Buried with the ship and its crew was all hope of peace, leaving behind a human turbulence beyond control by the hearts and minds of men. Spain and America, two proud countries, at last stood face to face.

Even at this moment, however, President McKinley still cherished some hope that Cuban independence could be won without further bloodshed. He began direct negotiations with Spain and exerted all the influence of his office through diplomatic channels, at the same time doing his best to hold down the public clamor. For instance, when Captain Sigsbee arrived in Washington in the last days of March, McKinley requested him not to attend a patriotic rally to which he had been invited as guest of honor and featured speaker. The Captain had become a national symbol and McKinley did not want the presence of the *Maine*'s commander to encourage frantic outcries for war from the thousands who would be present. Sigsbee agreed and was given, instead, a quiet reception by the National Geographic Society. Attending were the President, the Vice-President, the Secretary of the Navy, and many other distinguished officials.

Soon, though, McKinley had to admit that his diplomatic efforts were producing no results. Accordingly, with the backing of Congress, he publicly informed Spain that the United States would now insist on an immediate cease-fire in Cuba, and a complete end to all fighting, which must be guaranteed for six months. In that time, he hoped, the whole problem could be settled by negotiation and without any resort to arms. He demanded, as well, that the civilian population of the island — in particular the *Reconcentrados* — should be speedily relieved of hardship. Spain, acutely aware of the mood of America and appreciating the fact that McKinley was doing his best to hold the country in check, at last agreed to the armistice. Then she went even further and offered to grant Cuba complete self-government, retaining for herself only a commonwealth sovereignty over the island. It was the same arrangement, Spain pointed out, that existed between England and Canada.

As it turned out, however, neither of these concessions was able to halt the drift toward war. The insurgents, it was widely believed, would not agree to an armistice when they had complete independence within their grasp. And Spain, on its part, many said openly, was merely playing for time.

In addition, in one last effort to cool the runaway emotions that still surrounded the destruction of the *Maine*, the Spanish government suggested that the findings of both courts of inquiry should be submitted to an international tribunal of naval experts, chosen from other countries. But it was already too late for that. The United States had conducted her investigation with the utmost care, was satisfied with the decision, and in any case felt that she must maintain control of her own affairs. And obviously, to reopen such a tangled question in the prevailing atmosphere of world excitement would have been an invitation to chaos, leading to questionable results.

These were Spain's last moves toward preserving peace and beyond them she could not go. A country in which honor and dignity were fiercely upheld as the paramount qualities of life, Spain would not, in the face of threatened war, give up entirely a prize she had held for so many centuries and for which she had fought so long. It was the end of peaceful negotiations and both sides must have known it.

McKinley's Ultimatum

On April 11, President McKinley, under heavy pressure from a congressional war factor, set aside his call for an armistice and delivered an ultimatum: Spain must grant full freedom to Cuba or face prompt military action by the United States. The Spanish reply was to order the American ambassador out of Madrid. During the next few days, a flurry of last minute proposals and calls for peace flew wildly from country to country in Europe, and the Pope in Rome also offered his services as a mediator, but all ended in vain. On April 25, Congress declared war on Spain.

It was a conflict that the Spanish entered reluctantly and without heart, a war they knew they could not win. Even so, the eventual American victory was stunning, almost overwhelming in its speed and completeness. Within four months the brave but outclassed Spanish fleet had been destroyed, and the Spanish armies, fighting courageously but with a fatal expectation of defeat, had surrendered. Before the summer of 1898 was over, Cuba had her independence and America had taken a permanent place among the leading nations of the world.

Raising the *Maine*

The twentieth century dawned less than two years after the defeat of Spain, and with it memories of the *Maine* began to fade. As time passed, the ship remained at the bottom of Havana Harbor, her almost-hidden presence marked only by one protruding mast. Marine charts indicated her location almost as if she were a natural and permanent obstacle. Occasionally, someone would ask why the old wreck had not been cleared away, but nothing was done.

Then, in 1908, with the arrival of the tenth anniversary of the explosion, sentiment started to grow, especially among American patriotic organizations, that the wreck should at last be removed. It was suggested that the remains of the crew members still in the ship should be taken up for proper burial, and in any case the wreck had become a hazard to the increased traffic in Havana Harbor. Underlying these reasons, however, was a subtler and more potent factor — a nagging desire to settle the doubts and the persistent air of mystery that still clung round the tragedy. It was felt that if the wreck was raised and studied at leisure, something of significance might be discovered. Finally in 1910, Congress passed a bill authorizing the work, and setting up a new court of inquiry.

The task was a huge and complicated one and the methods proposed were finally reduced to two. One was to raise the ship bodily from the water by means of steel cables strung underneath and attached to powerful winches on ships stationed on either side. But this method, it was realized, would probably destroy much of the evidence by altering the relative positions of the ship's parts. The second plan was to sink around the vessel a cofferdam — a watertight enclosure — from which the water would be pumped out, thereby exposing the *Maine* to full view exactly as she had lain ever since the night she went down. This would allow an inspection team to crawl beneath the ship and make a minute study of every inch of the shattered hull. Though a cofferdam would take longer and be much more costly, it was really the only way to accomplish the job properly. The President (at that time William Howard Taft) declared that the cofferdam method would help to "strengthen the public confidence in the results," and he gave his approval.

Under supervision of the Army Engineer Corps, the work began early in 1911. Hollow steel cylinders, each one fifty feet in diameter, were sunk into the harbor bottom around the *Maine*, with the tops rising some five feet above the surface. When each cylinder was firmly in place it was packed full with earth and clay. After almost six months of work, twenty of these cylinders, strongly linked together, completely encircled the wreck, and the cofferdam was complete. The pumping out of the water began early in June and occupied another full month.

As the water level lowered day after day, the muddy, corroded, barnacle-encrusted ship gradually appeared, the forward section looking like some many-tentacled monster brought up from the depths. By August, the dam had been emptied down to the mud level, but the lower parts of the hull, especially toward the bow, had sunk some distance into the mud and this also had to be cleared

[49]

The wreck of the Maine rises to view again as water is pumped out of the cofferdam. She had lain on the bottom for fourteen years. The twisted bow is seen in the foreground, while the intact after section, with the mast still upright, is in the rear. (National Archives)

away, a process that required many more weeks. Finally, in November, the entire vessel was uncovered and the court of inquiry arrived to begin its inspection.

Measuring, testing, constantly referring to blueprints and plans, the experts spent nearly a month crawling around and underneath the hull. Many photographs were taken and a three-dimensional model was prepared showing the ship exactly as she lay. At last, on December 9, 1911, the court's verdict was submitted to President Taft and then released to the public.

The Second Court's Findings

"The Board finds," stated the report, "that the injuries to the bottom of the *Maine* were caused by the explosion of a low form of explosive exterior to the ship, between frames 28 and 21, strake B, port side. This resulted in igniting and exploding the contents of the six-inch reserve magazine. The more or less complete explosion of the contents of the remaining forward magazines followed. The magazine explosions resulted in the destruction of the vessel."

Thus the findings of the 1898 court of inquiry were confirmed, and the location of the first explosion, the exterior one, was located more precisely. The court also noted an important fact that had been overlooked earlier: the six-inch magazine had contained a large quantity of black powder, a type that was "more readily detonated by concussion." Because of this, the first explosion outside the ship's hull need not have been very large or powerful.

[51]

Americans were glad to have the original findings confirmed, but there was general disappointment that nothing had appeared to identify those responsible for the terrible deed. It had been hoped that pieces of the mine or the torpedo might be recovered, perhaps remains of a detonating cable, any little piece of evidence that would provide a clue. But there was nothing, and today, seventy years later, the mystery is still officially unsolved.

A number of theories have been proposed, involving both the Spanish and the Cuban insurrectionists, but the problem always reduces itself to one of method: how was the explosive placed beneath the ship? No answer to that question satisfies everyone, yet there are bits and pieces of evidence which, when brought together, supply a theory of at least reasonable probability. It points to the fact that the destruction of the *Maine* may have been both deliberate *and* accidental. (And this, interestingly enough, provides curious confirmation of Captain Sigsbee's feeling, expressed on the day of the explosion, that while the *Maine* had probably been destroyed by a mine, "it may have been done by accident.")

To begin with, there can be no doubt that someone set off an explosion beneath the ship. But it is absurd to think that it could have been a calculated move by the Spanish authorities, since that would have been purely senseless provocation, without purpose or design. And the same holds generally true for the suggestion that the culprits might have been a group of Spanish fanatics, acting inde-

The upright mainmast now stands in the National Cemetery at Arlington, Virginia, as part of a monument to the men who served aboard the Maine. *(National Archives)*

[52]

pendently. It is much more likely, as many people thought at the time, that the deed was done by a rabid band of Cuban rebels who hoped to throw the blame on the Spanish, inflame American opinion, and bring the United States actively into the struggle.

An objection to this theory is that the insurrectionists were not in a position in Havana to accomplish the task of placing a large mine under the ship or of firing a torpedo.

But there is another possible method, and it is even supported by an actual rumor which was current at the time of the sinking and which persisted for years. Two divers, it was said, operating out of a warehouse near the shore descended into the water by night, made their way to the *Maine*, and fixed a massive charge of dynamite to the hull. The dynamite, supposedly, was connected by insulated copper wire to the warehouse, from where it was later detonated. If Cuban rebels were responsible, however, it is most likely that they merely meant to damage the vessel, relying on the furor over the De Lome letter to compound the incident. Through miscalculation or ignorance, they put the dynamite beneath the ship's six-inch magazine, in which was stored the black powder so easily detonated by concussion. The resulting tragedy, then, would really have been an accident, unforeseen and unintended. If this is indeed what happened, it is not surprising that the truth went to the graves with the men who did it.

Borne on the shoulders of U.S. Marines, the last of the Maine's victims leave Havana to be brought home for burial. On the day the hulk of the Maine was buried at sea, thirty-four coffins which were supposed to contain the bones of sixty-four sailors were carried to the battleship North Carolina. Face superimposed on the photo is that of Father Chadwick, the Maine's chaplain, who said a solemn requiem mass over the ship's dead. Photo below shows sailors of the North Carolina hoisting the coffins aboard. These were the men who were buried in the Maine plot in Arlington Cemetery. Note old naval uniforms — blue collars on whites. (New York Public Library)

The Burial of the *Maine*

In February of 1912, workers began cutting the wreck apart with acetylene torches. It had been decided to separate the two halves of the ship, close off the after portion of the hull, and attempt to refloat it. If all went well, Congress directed, the derelict should be towed to sea and given an appropriate burial in honor of the men who had served on her.

By March, the wreckage of the bow had been cleared away and a new bulkhead had been affixed to the after section. Pumps pulled harbor water back into the cofferdam and as the level rose, the hull rose with it, riding lightly and evenly. Soon the remnant of the *Maine* was afloat once more on Havana Harbor.

On the day of the burial, two American warships, the cruiser *Birmingham* and the battleship *North Carolina*, arrived to escort the *Maine* to sea. As the nautical procession, joined by dozens of other boats large and small, wound slowly out of the harbor, eighty thousand Cubans lined the shores in silence. The big guns of Morro Castle boomed a salute every minute, and on its ramparts Cuban

soldiers stood at attention. The hulk, towed by a barge, had been decorated with hundreds of floral wreaths and her decks strewn with flowers; from her mast flew a large American flag.

Three miles outside Havana, the hulk was brought to a stop over a depth of six hundred fathoms and the processional fleet formed around her. A working party went aboard, opened the *Maine's* sea cocks and sluiceways, then left. While the men on the escort ships stood with bared heads, the *Maine* began to settle slowly in the slightly swelling waves. Then the American flag dipped beneath the surface; the stern lifted and slid under. From the deck of the *North Carolina* a bugle rang out, its clear, silvery notes sounding taps in a last farewell.

With her flag still flying and escort vessels standing by, the Maine *slides beneath the water's surface to disappear forever. (New York Public Library)*

Bibliography

Carleton, W., "The Funeral of the Maine." *Harper's Weekly*, (March 30, 1912).

Lackawanna Steel Co., *Raising the Wreck of the Maine*. N.Y., 1912.

Marshall, Gen. S. L. A., *The War to Free Cuba*. N.Y., 1912.

Mason, Gregory, *Remember the Maine*. Henry Holt & Co. N.Y., 1939.

Millis, Walter, *The Martial Spirit*. Houghton Mifflin, Boston, 1931.

Rea, George, "The Night of the Explosion in Havana." *Harper's Weekly*, (March 5, 1898).

"Report of the Naval Court on the Destruction of the Maine." *Scientific American*, (April 9, 1898).

Sigsbee, Charles, *The Maine*. The Century Co. N.Y., 1899.

Sigsbee, Charles, "My Story of the Maine." *Cosmopolitan*, (July-August, 1912).

Spear, John, *History of the U.S. Navy*. The Century Co. N.Y., 1908.

Swanberg, William, *Citizen Hearst*. New York: Charles Scribner's Sons, 1961.

"The Disaster to the Maine." *Scientific American*, (February 26, 1898).

Weems, John, *The Fate of the Maine*. Henry Holt & Co. N.Y., 1958.

Winkler, John, *William Randolph Hearst: A New Appraisal*. Hastings House. 1955.

Young, James, *The History of Our War with Spain*. J. R. Jones Co. Washington, 1899.

Index